TALES of TALIESIN

The MAGIC STORM

Based on a Welsh legend
Retold by Dawn Casey
Illustrated by Dante Ginerva

CHAPTER 1
A Singing Baby

On the crest of a wave, a basket bobbed. From inside the basket came a sound. Could it be humming? It sounded almost like singing.

Elphin heard it as he walked along the shore. He shaded his eyes and gazed along the waves. Yes, there was definitely something inside the basket.

Elphin waded into the water and scooped it up. He looked inside and gasped. A baby!

He stroked the baby's brow. "What a bright, bonny boy. I'll call you Taliesin."

The baby hummed happily.

"A singing baby!" Elphin laughed. "What a wonder!"

Elphin had a kind heart. He took the baby home and looked after him.

It was clear that Taliesin was no ordinary child, but Elphin loved him like his own son.

The baby Taliesin grew into a boy.
He loved running and jumping.
He loved swimming and leaping.
Most of all, he loved to sing.
But Taliesin was no ordinary boy.
His songs crackled with magic.

Every year, in mid-winter, the king held a Christmas feast. Elphin was always invited. When Taliesin was nine, he went too.

"Welcome to my castle!" boomed the king. "Is it not the greatest castle you've ever seen?"

Before Elphin could answer, the king began again. He boasted and he bragged. "My horses are the fastest. My knights are the bravest. And my singers are the best in the land."

Elphin smiled. "My son Taliesin loves singing too," he said proudly. "I think his songs are the best!"

"Nonsense!" roared the king. "A boy could never match *my* singers!"

Heinin, the chief singer, glared. "Sire, Elphin has insulted you. He deserves to be punished."

"Guards!" the king bellowed. "Throw this man into the dungeon!"

Elphin was dragged away in chains. While the king and his men ate and drank and laughed, Taliesin hid himself in a dark corner. One thought rang in his mind. "How can I save my father?"

CHAPTER 2

Wild Words

"Now!" said the king. "It is time for my singers to praise me."

Heinin came forward. As he walked past, Taliesin stuck out his bottom lip. He wobbled it with his finger. It made a noise.

"Bubba – bubba – bubba!"

Heinin bowed low. He was ready to
sing about how mighty the king was.
How marvellous. How magnificent.
He opened his mouth …

"BUBBA – BUBBA – BUBBA!"
The king's face turned red. "What!"
Heinin tried again. This time, his lips stuck
out. His nose screwed up. His eyes goggled.
"BUBBA – BUBBA – BUBBA!"

The king's face turned from red to purple. "Explain yourself!"

"Please, Sire," Heinin begged. "I am under a spell," and he pointed to Taliesin.

"You, boy!" thundered the king. "Who are you?"

Taliesin stood tall. "I am Taliesin. *I* am the best singer in the land. My father Elphin spoke no lie. So set him free."

The king snorted. "You? You're just a boy!" Taliesin answered, "I am young, but my songs are old." And he sang ...

"Old as the earth, deep as the seas, bright as the stars, wise as the trees."

Taliesin's words rang out. The king stared, open-mouthed.

"Now," said Taliesin, "will you set my father free?"

"No," said the king, "I will not."

"Very well," said Taliesin. "Then I will sing again."

And he sang a riddle.

"What is it that has no feet, yet runs over the seas?"

"What is it
that has no wings,
yet flies over the trees?"

"What is it,
as old as time,
that no one ever sees?"

17

As Taliesin sang, the king's men heard another sound.

A whisper. A whistle. A groaning. A growling.

Something was stirring.

Rushing and roaring, surging and soaring.

Louder and louder …

"Here's the answer to my riddle,"
Taliesin laughed. "The wind!"
The castle doors burst open as the
wind whirled in.

CHAPTER 3
Storm

Cups clattered. Jugs shattered.

The king ducked as a pot swept past and knocked his crown to the ground.

The wild wind tore the swords from the knights' waists. It jangled and clanged and swirled and spun them.

The knights swerved and dodged.

The king hid under the table, but the table took off and smashed into the wall. And all the while the wind lashed and crashed and hurled and howled.

The king cowered. "Guards!" he ordered. "Bring Elphin here!"

Elphin stood before them, still bound in chains.

"Now," Taliesin commanded, "wild winds blow!"

The winds ripped Elphin's chains apart.

With a sigh, the winds were gone and Elphin stood free.

The king's hair stuck out in all directions. He flattened it down and put on his crown. "Taliesin," he said. "You *are* the best. I declare that from this day forth, you will be known as Taliesin, King of Singers."

So Elphin and Taliesin walked home
together through the trees. The wind ruffled
their hair, and Taliesin was singing.